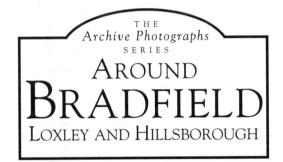

THE
Archive Photographs
SERIES

AROUND
BRADFIELD
LOXLEY AND HILLSBOROUGH

BRADFIELD
Musical Festival.

On Whit-Monday, the 23d Day of May, 1825,

WILL BE PERFORMED AT

BRADFIELD CHURCH,

A Grand Selection of

SACRED
MUSIC,

From the Works of Handel, Haydn, &c. &c.

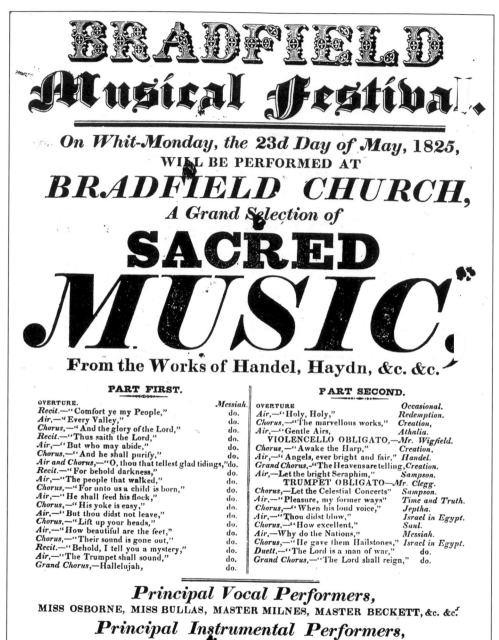

PART FIRST.	
OVERTURE.	Messiah.
Recit.—"Comfort ye my People,"	do.
Air,—"Every Valley,"	do.
Chorus,—"And the glory of the Lord,"	do.
Recit.—"Thus saith the Lord,"	do.
Air,—"But who may abide,"	do.
Chorus,—"And he shall purify,"	do.
Air and Chorus,—"O, thou that tellest glad tidings,"	do.
Recit.—"For behold darkness,"	do.
Air,—"The people that walked,"	do.
Chorus,—"For unto us a child is born,"	do.
Air,—"He shall feed his flock,"	do.
Chorus,—"His yoke is easy,"	do.
Air,—"But thou didst not leave,"	do.
Chorus,—"Lift up your heads,"	do.
Air,—"How beautiful are the feet,"	do.
Chorus,—"Their sound is gone out,"	do.
Recit.—"Behold, I tell you a mystery,"	do.
Air,—"The Trumpet shall sound,"	do.
Grand Chorus,—Hallelujah,	do.

PART SECOND.	
OVERTURE	Occasional.
Air,—"Holy, Holy,"	Redemption.
Chorus,—"The marvellous works,"	Creation,
Air,—"Gentle Airs,	Athalia.
VIOLENCELLO OBLIGATO,—Mr. Wigfield.	
Chorus,—"Awake the Harp,"	Creation.
Air,—"Angels, ever bright and fair,"	Handel.
Grand Chorus,-"The Heavens are telling,	Creation.
Air,—Let the bright Seraphim,"	Sampson.
TRUMPET OBLIGATO—Mr. Clegg.	
Chorus,—Let the Celestial Concerts"	Sampson.
Air,—"Pleasure, my former ways"	Time and Truth.
Chorus,—"When his loud voice,"	Jeptha.
Air,—"Thou didst blow,"	Israel in Egypt.
Chorus,—"How excellent,"	Saul.
Air,—Why do the Nations,"	Messiah.
Chorus,—"He gave them Hailstones,"	Israel in Egypt.
Duett,—"The Lord is a man of war,"	do.
Grand Chorus,—"The Lord shall reign,"	do.

Principal Vocal Performers,

MISS OSBORNE, MISS BULLAS, MASTER MILNES, MASTER BECKETT, &c. &c.

Principal Instrumental Performers,

Leader of the Band, MR. WIGFIELD, JUN.—Trumpet, MR. CLEGG,—Bassoon, MR. DAWSON,—Trombone, MR. SMITH, &c. &c. Assisted by the Gentlemen of the Amateur Concert.

Admission,—Chancel, 2s.—Gallery, 2s.—Body of the Church, 1s.

Tickets to be had on or before the Day of Performance, at any of the three Inns; also, Books of the Performance at Sixpence each.

Doors to be Opened at One o'Clock, and the Performance to begin precisely at Two.

The BAND and CHORUSSES will be full, Grand, and Effective.

Albion Office: Printed by C. & W. Thompson, Sheffield.

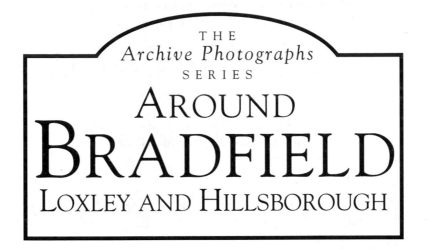

THE
Archive Photographs
SERIES

AROUND
BRADFIELD
LOXLEY AND HILLSBOROUGH

Compiled by
Malcolm Nunn

CHALFORD

First published 1996
Reprinted 1997
Copyright © Malcolm Nunn, 1996

The Chalford Publishing Company
St Mary's Mill, Chalford,
Stroud, Gloucestershire, GL6 8NX

ISBN 0 7524 0671 X

Typesetting and origination by
The Chalford Publishing Company
Printed in Great Britain by
Redwood Books, Trowbridge

Workmen employed by Thos. Marshalls, Storrs Fireclay Works, Loxley c. 1934.

Contents

Oughtibridge Hospital parade to raise funds for local hospitals, 1911.

Acknowledgements

Most of the pictures and illustrations used in this edition have been taken from my own collection amassed over many years. However, I would like to thank those that have contributed precious family photographs, helped with valuable information or simply allowed me to share in some of their memories of the area.

The Bradfield Parish Council; Bradfield Historical Society; *The Yorkshire Post*; Stannington Historical Society. Those individuals who have contributed include: E. Goddard, J. Goddard, P. Manley, B. Manley, H. Burley, V. Crapper, A. Emsall, J. Bishop, P. Walker, G. Harper, D. Harper, M. Robinson, M. Satterthwaite, S. Mallinson, M. Hallam, M. Helliwell.

Introduction

The Civil Parish of Bradfield is the largest in England covering over 35,000 acres and has a population of over 15,000. The main villages are High and Low Bradfield, Loxley, Stannington, Oughtibridge, Worrall, Dungworth, along with many much smaller hamlets.

Some of the communities on the fringes of the Parish – Hillsborough, Wadsley, Malin Bridge – have also been included to provide a comprehensive picture of life in the north west of Sheffield.

Bradfield consists of three areas: Low and High Bradfield and Bradfield Dale. Low Bradfield has been an attraction for visitors over the years especially in summertime during the cricket season. High Bradfield is dominated by St Nicholas church which dates back to 1487; Bradfield Dale is popular with ramblers particularly around Adgen, Dale Dyke and Strines reservoirs. The whole area is a rural idyll of picturesque moorland. Bradfield also had a workhouse – built at High Bradfield in 1769 to house the poor and homeless of the parish it remained in exsistence for almost eighty years until the abolition of the poor laws. The workhouse buildings were eventually converted to homes in the 1870s and were again refurbished in the early 1990s. A cupboard discovered in 1954 in one of these premises (but not opened until 1970) was found to contain 10,000 documents relating to all aspects of the workhouse. Most of these papers were catalogued by the Bradfield Historical Society (a few of which appear in this book) and today reside at Bradfield Parish Council offices.

The Ewden Valley, which includes Brightholmlee, contains two reservoirs built in the 1920s – Morehall and Broomhead. The latter was not put into full operational use until 1933 due to continual leakage (Yorkshire Water take note). The area consists of many farms and agricultural dwellings; the old buildings at Brightholmlee are of particular note, some date from the fourteenth century. The parish also has several 'cruck barns' but at Brightholmlee, High Lea Farm is a 'cruck house' – a very unusual feature.

Wadsley's name is derived from the Old English *Wadde's Leah* and came under the control of the De Wadsley family during the nineteenth century. The area was famed for the production of knives known locally as 'Wadsley Flat Backs'. Wadsley Village consisted of many small one-up and one-down dwellings – the majority of which disappeared during the clearances of the 1960s and 1970s to be replaced by modern housing. Above the village stands Wadsley and Loxley Common where stone and gannister quarrying took place up to sixty years ago and on Loxley Edge stood an ancient gibbett last used in 1783 to hang the body of Frank Fearns following his execution at York for the murder of Nathan Andrews at nearby Kirkedge.

The main industrial areas (and the consequent residential and commercial zones) formed along the banks of the rivers Loxley and Don. Hillsborough took its name from Lord Downshire of Hillsborough in County Down in 1779 as a tribute to that particular noble. This particular suburb has grown enormously over the last two centuries and is now home to over twenty thousand people as well as such 'organisations' as Sheffield Wednesday Football Club and the Sheffield Speedway. Malin Bridge suffered devastating damage in the floods of 1864 and the original Yew Tree Inn was used as a temporary mortuary for victims. Owlerton grew up around Owlerton Hall (which dates back to the fifthteenth century) and stood at the junction of the Penistone Road and the Bradfield Road.

Loxley formed as pocket industries along the banks of the River Loxley; the residential area followed at the turn of the last century. The water powered wheels on the River Loxley were severely damaged or destroyed in the 1864 flood but there area still many reminders of the valley industries – Mill Dams, Head Goyts, Tail Goyts and Weirs. Little Matlock Rolling Mills is still in use today and, although now powered by electricity, the old water wheel can be seen adjacent to the site. Refractory works were also prominent producing furnace bricks for the many steelworks in Sheffield and providing employment for a great number of locals. The downturn in the fortunes of the steel industry brought a consequent decline in the need for refractory materials. Today the industry which had employed hundreds has only a handful of employees.

Oughtibridge was an industrial area which grew up beside the River Don, the most prominent and largest employers being the Peter Dixon's paper mill and the Silica brickworks (now closed). The population grew with the success of these industries and Oughtibridge formed a major connection on the now defunct Sheffield to Manchester (via Woodhead) railway line. Above the valley the village of Worrall supplied many workers for local industries and services including the Middlewood Hospital, Wadsley gannister mines and the Loxley refractory works. Many of the original cottages were pulled down in the late 1960s during the clearances.

In the south of the parish Dungworth and Storrs were and are mainly rural and agricultural villages although there is some evidence of coal mining in the last century and clay mining for the refractories on the Loxley Valley. Local traditions are still strong in the villages: 'caking night' is held the week before bonfire night and Christmas Carols are sung at the Royal Hotel in Dungworth. On the south-east corner of the parish Stannington is the largest village (in terms of population). The pictures shown on the village were kindly loaned by the Stannington History Society for which the author would like to give due thanks.

I hope that this nostalgic tour of the area will be enjoyed by all. The easy pace of life presented here may have vanished but these pictures provide a thread to the past and are a part of our heritage. Everyone who lives or works in the area will recognise streets, buildings or even faces and the dramatic changes that have been wrought in such a short span of history.

One
High and Low Bradfield

Low Bradfield Village and the Smithy Bridge in the *c*. 1948.

Low Bradfield Village in 1914. Burnside Cottages can be seen in the centre; the Cornmill which was destroyed by fire in 1940 is on the right.

Low Bradfield looking toward Burnside Cottages in 1915. The buildings in the foreground are the Blacksmiths and Joiners shop.

Woodfall Lane in Low Bradfield c. 1925. The lane is known locally as The Street. The Cross Inn on the left is now a private residence while the shop on the right is now the village post office and store.

The Sands at Low Bradfield in 1912. The cottages on the left were demolished during the 1960s – the main house having gone several years before that. Cattle are still driven across the stream into fields beyond for grazing.

Kirk Steps at Low Bradfield in 1915. The bridge crosses Agden Beck and the steps and footpath lead to High Bradfield.

Fairhouse Cottages at Low Bradfield in 1972 just before demolition to make way for the bus turning circle.

Fair House Farm at Low Bradfield *c.* 1920. The farm is one of the oldest buildings in the area (dating from the 1630s) and was originally called Swinden House.

FILTER HOUSES. LOW BRADFIELD. 737   FURNISS SHEFFIELD

The Filter Houses near Low Bradfield were built in 1913 and further extended in 1953. The site is now closed following the construction of the Loxley Valley water treatment works in 1995.

The Wesleyan chapel at Low Bradfield in 1911. The chapel opened in 1899 and replaced the building on the right which had been used for worship since 1817 but is today the offices of the Bradfield Parish Council. The chapel closed in 1993 and has now been sold for residential use.

The Wesleyan Chapels at Low Bradfield in 1911. The small walled enclosure in front of the bridge is a sheep wash in which cattle were cleaned before going to auction at the nearby Plough Inn.

High Bradfield Village in 1912 – a scene dominated by St Nicholas church which dates from Saxon times. The farm buildings on the left have since been demolished and are now the site of the car park for the Old Horn's Inn.

Towngate at High Bradfield in 1912. These cottages were formerly workhouses built around 1760 and were modernised in the late 1980s and early 1990s to provide private residences.

Watch House, Bradfield
M&S. 1842

'The Watch House' at High Bradfield. The house was built in 1745 as a place from which to guard newly buried bodies in the churchyard. There are only two or three houses of this type still in existence in the country.

St Nicholas church at High Bradfield *c.* 1912. This famous Yorkshire church dates from Saxon times; although nothing of that period remains following several rebuilds, the oldest section is from 1487.

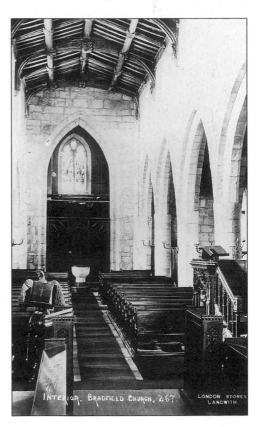

The interior of St Nicholas church in 1912.

This ancient cross was dug up in the fields near Cross Farm at Low Bradfield. It is thought to be a waymarker of ancient, probably Celtic or Saxon, origin. It was placed in St Nicholas church at High Bradfield in 1886.

Bailey Hill at High Bradfield in 1911. This old Bailey is at the rear of the church. Many Baileys were built by the Normans after the Conquest of 1066 mainly by forced local labour; these fortresses could then be used as a base to subdue a hostile local population. Note the people in full Sunday best at the top of the mound.

The Rectory at High Bradfield *c*. 1910. A part of this building has now been separated for private residential use.

A view of Bradfield Dale in 1915. Agden reservoir is in the foreground, Dale Dyke is in the centre and Strines Reservoir can be seen in the distance. The moorland on the horizon forms the border between Yorkshire and Derbyshire.

A view of Agden reservoir, built in 1869, from the top of the old Bailey *c.* 1912. The small hamlet on the right is Smallfield.

The waste water weir at Agden reservoir in 1915 – excess water here is used to keep Agden Beck flowing.

The culvert around Agden reservoir helps to send the drained water to be purified at the water treatment works.

Agden House in 1911. The building, which was over 300 years old, was demolished in the early 1970s.

Hallfield House in Bradfield Dale was constructed in Elizabethan times and was for many years the home of the Greaves family; later Earl Fitzwilliam owned the property. After falling derelict for some twenty years the property has since undergone an extensive refurbishment.

Dale Dyke reservoir *c.* 1911. An inscription shows it was the cause of the Sheffield Flood of 1864. The reservoir was later rebuilt with a new embankment sited 200 yards upstream with the water capacity reduced by a third. This particular view is today restricted by trees which have grown up beside the embankment.

Reservoir Inn in Bradfield Dale *c.* 1920 is now called the Haychatter Inn. It was originally a farmhouse and dates back to the seventeenth century. During the construction of Dale Dyke reservoir in the 1850s and 1860s it was a popular beerhouse with locals and workers alike.

Annett Bridge in Bradfield Dale replaced an older construction which was the first obstacle swept away during the flood of 1864.

A vingette card of 1938 showing Strines Inn in Bradfield Dale. The Inn on Mortimer Road dates from the late sixteenth century.

Strines Inn, *c.* 1920, was known at one time as 'Taylors Arms'.

Dam Flask reservoir was built in 1867 but did not become operational until 1896. It supplies many of the factories along the route into Sheffield.

A view of Dam Flask and the Loxley Valley in 1930 from Oakes Lane.

A Sunday school outing passes Dam Flask in 1920. This group probably attended a Whitsuntide gathering in Hillsborough Park.

A Bradfield Christmas card of 1920 showing various views of the area and probably issued by St Nicholas chruch.

Haycutting near Dyson House *c*. 1920. Low Bradfield can be seen in the background.

Agriculture is the mainstay of the Bradfield area and haymaking was a feature of the rural life.

The High Bradfield churchbell ringers in 1920 consisted almost entirely of the Gillott family.

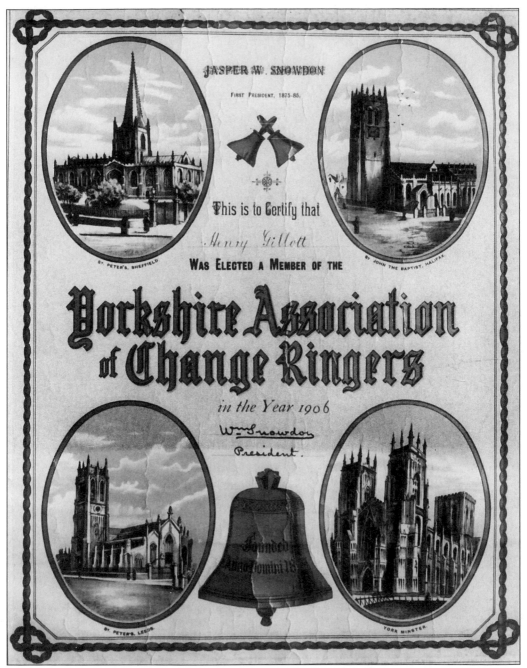

The certificate awarded to Henry Gillott in 1906 by the Yorkshire Association of Change Ringers.

Bradfield Agricultural Show in the early 1950s was probably one of the last before the tradition died out.

A staged village wedding in 1928 by the members of the Bradfield Village Mothers Union.

'Stocking Johnny' was a regular visitor to Bradfield walking from Honley and stopping overnight at farms on the way. His real name was Mr Burdett and he carried goods for sale in Bradfield in two traiangular shoulder bags. These included: stockings, knickers, shoelaces, buttons, cottons, threads, pins and even medicines and remedies for coughs and colds.

A group outside the Haychatter Inn in 1928. They are back row, left to right: -?-, Joel Buckley, Harry Crawshaw, Ellis Uttley (landlord), Paddy ? , -?-. Front row: Colin Hopkins, Fred Mathers, Charlie Elliott, Henry Booker-Elliott, Ernest Waterhouse, Billy Crawshaw.

Mr Jack Yelland and his waggonette with workmen for the new filter house at Bradfield in 1913. Before the days of regular bus service Jack also provided similar transport for people going to Hillsborough.

A church garden party at High Bradfield in 1956.

High Bradfield school class of 1912. Back row, left to right: Teddy Horsfield, ? Hulley, Charlie Morton, Nellie Gillott, Lizzie Armitage, Annie Helliwell, Frank Parker, Bernard Hawke, Percy Shaw. Middle row: Rowland Carnelly, May Wragg, Connie Gillott, Annie Sanderson, Mary Morton, Gladys Buckley, Alice Buckley, Alice Wragg, Wilton Morton. Front row: Billy Gillott, Fred Sanderson, Billy Hawke, Florrie Gillott, Sam Firth, ? Firth, Jonte Gillott, ? Hulley, Cissie Wragg, Henry Gillott.

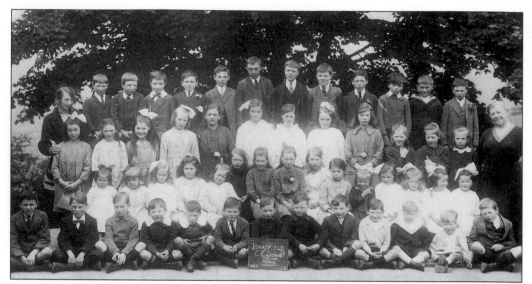

High Bradfield school in 1922. Those identified so far include Bernard Ellis, Leonard Rowett, William Marsden, Cyril Broadhead, John Thorpe, Henry Hunt, Clem Elliott, George Fretwell, Mabel Hadfield (teacher), Phyllis Bramall, Bertha Makin, Doris Bramall, Mary Checkley, Annie Robinson, Ada Broadhead, Zillah Shepherd (teacher).

Low Bradfield school in 1916. Back row, left to right: George Perkins, Gervase Worrall, Olive Bramall, Phyllis Hadfield, May Crawshaw, Joe Hadfield. Middle row: Gerald Worrall, Edna Elliott, Phyllis Sanderson, Janet Elliott, Una Elliott, Lillian Bramall, Frank Fretwell. Front row: Mark Elliott, John Hopkins, Lily Wilson, Florence Siddons, Marian Mudford, Alf Elliott, Sam Fretwell.

Low Bradfield school in 1929. Back row, left to right: Arthur Shepherd, Ellis Uttley, Leonard Shepherd, Verdon Elliott, Hadyn Elliott, Gordon Elliott. Top middle row: Myrtle Hopkins, Helen Shepherd, Megan Shepherd, Elsie Sampson, Connie Green, Ida Shepherd, Edna Fretwell, Theodore Laing. Middle row: Renee Hawley, Leonard Hadfield, Alwyn Dearden, Elsie Hawke, Cynthia Smith, Edith Shepherd, Mary Shepherd, Mary Buckley, Lorna Green, Joyce Laing, Kathleen Crawshaw, Peggy Green, Fred Shepherd, Ralph Robinson. Front middle row: LenaWragg, Ruth Robinson, Florence Parkin, Doreen Crapper, Dorothy Hadfield, Betty Elliott, Kathleen Green. Front row: Alwyn Elliott, Willis Hawke, Eric Elliott, Fred Sampson, Arthur Elliott, Ronnie Sanderson, Leonard Crawshaw, George Shaw.

Low Bradfield school 1951. Back row, left to right: Mrs Cooper, Harry Hartley, Stephen Shepherd, David Elliott, George Marshall, David Broadhead, David Sanderson, Neville Ashton, Mrs Ivy Hammond. Top middle row: Elizabeth Davies, Margaret Oades, Ellen Fretwell, Anne Uttley, Lena Thorpe, Dorothy Dixon, Patricia Elliott. Middle row: Jennifer Tyson, Jean Siddall, Irene Merryman, Christine Elliott, Barbara Fretwell, Janet Dixon, Carol Thompson. Front middle row: Michael King, David Leader, James Hammond, Robert Leader, Andrew King, Brain Fretwell, John Powell, Keith Wainwright. Front row: Wilfred Barrell, Jean Hague, Patricia Leader, Jill Livsey, Margaret Merryman, Anne Eaton, Janet Greenwood, Cedric Wragg.

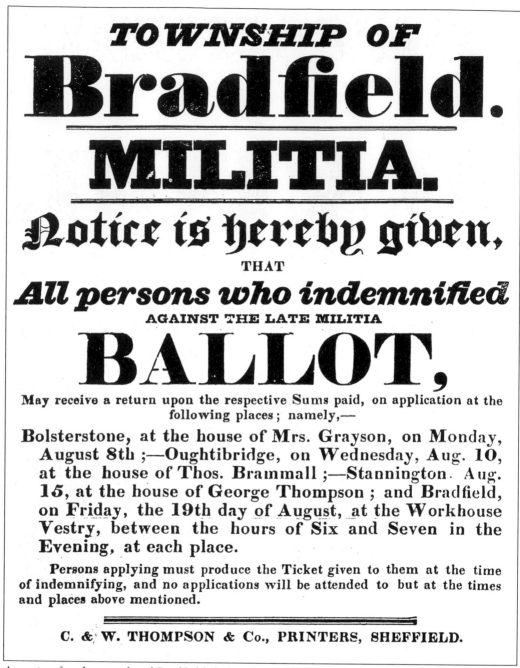

TOWNSHIP OF
Bradfield.
MILITIA.

Notice is hereby given,

THAT

All persons who indemnified

AGAINST THE LATE MILITIA

BALLOT,

May receive a return upon the respective Sums paid, on application at the following places; namely,—

Bolsterstone, at the house of Mrs. Grayson, on Monday, August 8th ;—Oughtibridge, on Wednesday, Aug. 10, at the house of Thos. Brammall ;—Stannington. Aug. 15, at the house of George Thompson ; and Bradfield, on Friday, the 19th day of August, at the Workhouse Vestry, between the hours of Six and Seven in the Evening, at each place.

Persons applying must produce the Ticket given to them at the time of indemnifying, and no applications will be attended to but at the times and places above mentioned.

C. & W. THOMPSON & Co., PRINTERS, SHEFFIELD.

A notice for the people of Bradfield dating from the early nineteenth century. Many of the following documents were discovered in a cupboard in cottages that had formerly served as the workhouse. Copies of these are kept at the offices of the Bradfield Parish Council.

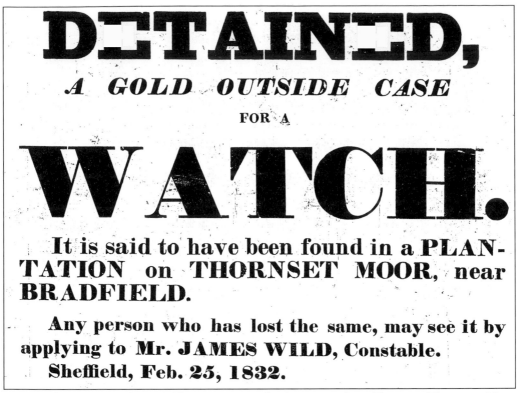

DETAINED,

A GOLD OUTSIDE CASE

FOR A

WATCH.

It is said to have been found in a PLAN-TATION on THORNSET MOOR, near BRADFIELD.

Any person who has lost the same, may see it by applying to Mr. JAMES WILD, Constable.

Sheffield, Feb. 25, 1832.

A notice from the local constable announcing the discovery of a gold case at Thornsett Moor in 1832.

A register of electors notice for Bradfield in 1832.

W. R.

Township
OF
BRADFIELD.

We hereby give Notice, that we shall, on or before the last day of July in this year, make out a List of all Persons entitled to Vote in the Election of a KNIGHT OR KNIGHTS OF THE SHIRE, for the West Riding of the County of York, in respect of Property situate wholly or in part within this Township ; and all Persons so entitled, are hereby required to deliver or to transmit to us, at the Vestry Office, Bradfield, on or before the 20th day of August in this year, a claim in writing, containing their Christian Name and Surname, their place of abode, the nature of their Qualification, and the Name of the Street, Lane, or other like Place, wherein the Property in respect of which they Claim to Vote is situated ; and if the Property be not situated in any Street, Lane, or other like place, then such Claim must describe the Property by the Name by which it is usually known, or by the Name of the Tenant occupying the same ; and each of such Persons so Claiming, must also at the same time pay to us the Sum of One Shilling.

Persons omitting to deliver or transmit such Claim, or to make such Payment, will be excluded from the Register of Voters for the said West Riding of the County of York.

Joseph Ashby
John Wood   } Overseers of the Poor
George Creswick   } of the Township of
Henry Armitage   } Bradfield.

BRADFIELD VESTRY OFFICE,
July 24, 1832.

C. & W. THOMPSON & Co., PRINTERS, SHEFFIELD.

TOWNSHIP OF
BRADFIELD.

NOTICE IS HEREBY GIVEN,
THAT A PUBLIC

MEETING

Will be held at the Workhouse, in Bradfield, on

WEDNESDAY,

THE 26th DAY OF MARCH INSTANT,
AT THREE O'CLOCK IN THE AFTERNOON,
To make out a LIST of PERSONS fit and proper to serve the office of

OVERSEERS OF THE POOR,

FOR THE YEAR ENSUING ;

Also GUARDIANS of the POOR will be nominated at the said Meeting. Also a SURVEYOR will be appointed for the Parish Road, in Wisewood. Also will be Let by Public Tender, the supplying of the Workhouse with Coals, for one year. Also the Ashes and Manure to be made at the Workhouse, during the ensuing year, will be sold by Public Tender.

And TAKE NOTICE, that all Persons who have any demand against the present Overseers, are requested to send in their Account, that the same may be examined, and if found correct, discharged.

And the RATE PAYERS who have not paid their Rates, are earnestly requested to pay the same on or before Monday, the 24th day of March Instant, as all Persons in Arrear after that day, will be summoned without further notice.

BY ORDER,

W. GUELDER, Assistant Overseer.

Bradfield Workhouse, March 10, 1845.]   [BLURTON, PRINTER, SHEFFIELD.

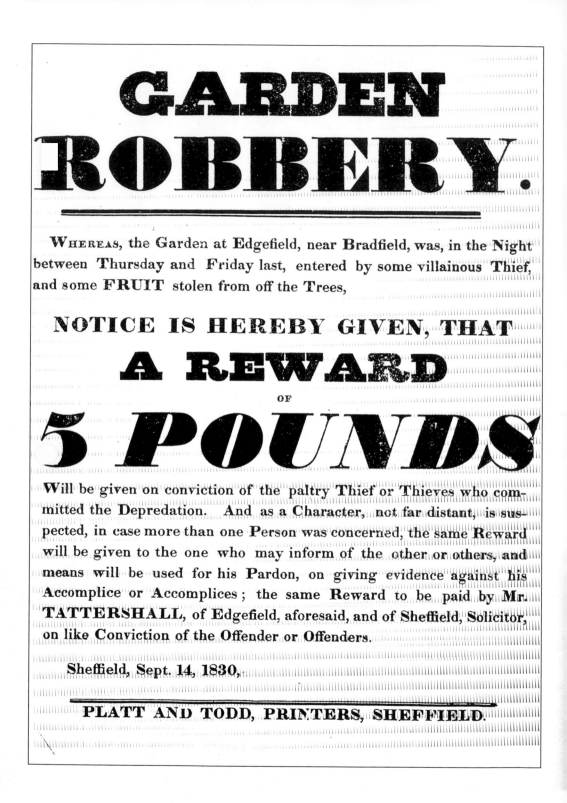

GARDEN ROBBERY.

WHEREAS, the Garden at Edgefield, near Bradfield, was, in the Night between Thursday and Friday last, entered by some villainous Thief, and some **FRUIT** stolen from off the Trees,

NOTICE IS HEREBY GIVEN, THAT

A REWARD

OF

5 POUNDS

Will be given on conviction of the paltry Thief or Thieves who committed the Depredation. And as a Character, not far distant, is suspected, in case more than one Person was concerned, the same Reward will be given to the one who may inform of the other or others, and means will be used for his Pardon, on giving evidence against his Accomplice or Accomplices; the same Reward to be paid by Mr. TATTERSHALL, of Edgefield, aforesaid, and of Sheffield, Solicitor, on like Conviction of the Offender or Offenders.

Sheffield, Sept. 14, 1830,

PLATT AND TODD, PRINTERS, SHEFFIELD.

Two
Dungworth and Storrs

A view over Load Brook. Thomas Wragg's factory at Load Brook closed in 1957 and very little evidence remains of its existence.

Dungworth village shop *c.* 1910. For over forty years this shop was referred to as 'Harper's Shop' after the family who owned it. The premises closed in 1970.

Dungworth Hall *c.* 1930 was built in the eighteenth century. Today these premises have been divided into three dwellings and are known as Padley Cottages.

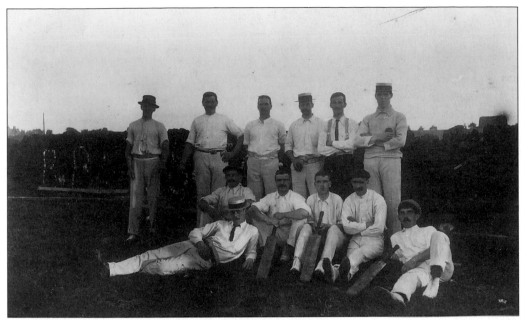
Dungworth Cricket team in the Royal playing fields in 1910.

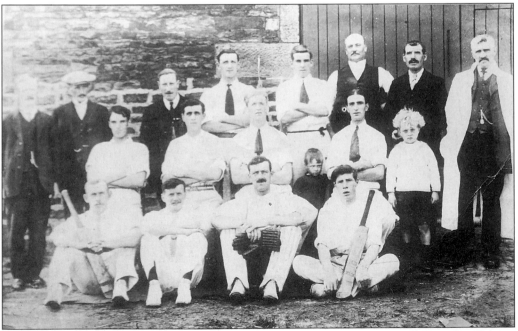
Dungworth Hilltop Cricket team *c.* 1900 outside the George Inn. The landlord of the George, Abner Thompson, is at position number six on the back row.

Petticoats and hobnail boots are *de rigeur* in this 1919 picture of Dungworth school.

Dungworth Junior and Infant school 1936-1937. Back row, left to right: Aubrey Elliott, Eric Baxter, Doran Crapper, Willis Harper, Roland Hague, Newton Ronksley, Billy Hallam. Top middle row: Rhoda Bramall, Dorothy Butcher, Pamela Harper, Cynthia Harper, Florence Andrew, Freda Crapper, Jean Gray. Bottom middle row: Irene Coldwell, Enid Fretwell, Eileen Drabble, -?-, Nancy Crapper. Front row: Cecil Coldwell, Vivian Crapper, Brian Wagstaffe.

Dungworth Junior and Infant school class 1934-35. Back row, left to right: Jean Gray, Mary Hall, Dorothy Butcher, Eileen Drabble, -?-, Enid Fretwell. Front row: Willis Harper, Doran Crapper, Brian Wagstaffe, Eric Baxter, Aubrey Elliott, Roland Hague.

The Dungworth Knurr and Spell team outside the Royal Hotel *c*. 1919. The basics of this sport were simple: a small ceramic ball was launched upwards from a spring trap whereupon a 'batter' would attempt to hit it as far as possible by means of a long wooden stick with a iron block on the end. In this team are back row, left to right: -?-, Jack Hawley, -?-, Harry Green, Albert Harper, Allan Gray, -?-. Front row: ? Fretwell, Ernest Wragg, Charles Green, Hedley Green, -?-, ? Emsall.

An outdoor chapel sermon in the yard of Greenfold Farm in Dungworth *c*. 1926.

A view over Storrs Bridge from Storrs *c.* 1932. On the right of the picture is Claremont House; Swifts Rolling mills and house are in the centre with workers cottages on the left.

The old Sunday school at Storrs is now a private residence – it was built in 1821 and closed in 1884 when the new chapel opened.

Chapel cottages at Storrs were built over 200 years ago. The original building was joined by a further building on the left – a feint brick line denotes the two separate parts. A cutlers shop operated at the rear at one time.

Storrs village shop closed in the 1960s and is now a private residence.

Storrs chapel was built in 1884 and closed in 1975 when it become a private residence.

Three
Stannington

J. & J. Dyson's Refractory 'Griff Works' premises on the Stopes Road at Stannington.

J. & J. Dyson, steam waggon at Stannington *c*. 1900.

The Queen's Hotel *c*. 1905. Mrs Milner and her mother can be seen in the doorway of the hotel which once served as Stannington Police station. Today the building is a private residence.

A rare picture of the old Methodist chapel before it was replaced on the same site by the present building.

The Methodist chapel, Knowle Top c. 1910.

Workmen and a collection of interested children at Knowle Top school as land is cleared for the graveyard *c.* 1905 .

A view of Uppergate from Knowle Top, a site known locally as 'between the fields'. The Post Office is on the right and the Hare and Hounds is third on the left.

The Hare and Hounds public house on Uppergate Road was demolished in the late 1960s and a replacement built on Church Street.

The unveiling of the War Memorial to the servicemen of the Great War 1914-1918 at Stannington in 1921.

A view over Uppergate taken from Nethergate in the 1930s.

Thrales buses outside the Crown and Glove Inn *c.* 1925. The Thrale bus service ran from Malin Bridge to Stannington and Bradfield. Pictured here are, left to right: H. Thrale, C. Holmes, A. Pickering, B. Gillott.

Knowle Top on the Stannington Road *c.* 1905. The Peacock Inn is on the right next to the Stannington blacksmiths.

Robin Hood Inn, Little Matlock *c.* 1910. This area was reputed to be the birthplace of the infamous Robin Hood or Robin of Loxley. The woodlands below the inn were designed by Thos. Halliday whose intent was to create water gardens and flower beds in which the gentry of Sheffield could wander. He named the area Little Matlock as he believed it similar in appearance to Matlock in Derbyshire.

Workmen of Henry Gosney and Sons, Rivelin Glen lorries *c.* 1910. Left to right: Arthur Gosney, John Edward Gosney, -?-, -?-, Bill Allison, Harry Allison, Tommy Booth, William Allison.

Stannington Boys Club football team during the 1937-1938 season.

Class four at the Stannington Church Day school *c.* 1905.

Four
Hillsborough
Malin Bridge and Owlerton

Malin Bridge and the Loxley Valley c. 1908. The bridge in the foreground is Stannington Road bridge; the large chinmey belongs to Wisewood Forge which was demolished in the 1960s.

Malin Bridge c. 1910. La Plata Works is in the foreground, Dykes Lane can be seen towards the right with St Mark's church and Malin Bridge school on either side of the road. The Wisewood estate has since been built on the ground to the left of this picture.

Malin Bridge corn mill c. 1915. The mill has had a varied life. For many years it was owned by Germain Wilson and was a carpentry and joiners shop before serving as a corn mill until the 1960s when it became an electrical warehouse. Today the building is used as a Cantonese restaurant.

Mouse Hole Forge at Malin Bridge produced anvils, for many years with the stamp of a mouse for identification. The remains of this forge has been preserved by the present owners.

The Hillsborough Inn c. 1910 was closed in the early 1960s and was subsequently converted into shops.

A horse-drawn tram stands outside the Hillsborough Inn on Hillsborough Corner in 1895. The horse-drawn tram was used in the area until 1902 when the electric version arrived on the streets.

Hillsborough Corner c. 1920. The building on the left has since had another floor added and is now Greenwood's shop. The second building is still recognisable as Shakespeare Inn and the third building is now the site of the Hillsborough precinct and Wilkinson DIY stores.

Hillsborough *c.* 1920. The white buildings on the left were demolished in 1993 to make way for the Sheffield Supertram.

Middlewood Road near to the junction with Dykes Hall Road Junction. This particular row of houses were demolished to make way for the Hillsborough Co-operative stores.

The junction of Middlewood Road and Dyke Hall Road at Hillsborough *c.* 1900.

The junction of Middlewood Road, Parkside Road, Willis Road and Wadsley Lane *c.* 1910 was the site of the tram terminus before it was extended into Middlewood.

H.A. Lingard's ironmongery store on Middlewood Road *c.* 1905. It was one of the shops owned by the Sheffield Company and today it is the site of a pork butchers.

Park Hotel was built on Wadsley Lane in 1908 and this picture was taken a few years after.

LEPPINGS LA, STEPPING STONES

The Lepping Stones at Owlerton *c.* 1890. These stones were replaced by the Leppings Lane Road Bridge and were situated, approximately, on the site of the new footbridge on the route to Sheffield Wednesday Football Club.

The five arches railway bridge carries the now defunct Sheffield to Manchester (via Woodhead) line. It is difficult to envisage this scene today, the centre arch of the bridge now straddles the Sheffield outer ring road ! The house on the far left is still a private residence.

Old workers cottages on Owlerton Green *c.* 1920.

HILLSBRO PARK, SHEFFIELD.   W. OLIVER, SHEFFIELD.   N.º 10

This beautifully ornate bandstand in Hillsborough Park was demolished in the 1950s.

Hillsborough Barracks *c.* 1910. The barracks opened in 1849 for artillery and infantry regiments and eventually closed in 1932. The majority of the site is today part of the Morrison's supermarket.

Hillsborough c. 1910. The Soldier's Home on Langsett Road which has for many years been a boys club.

Hillsborough and Malin Bridge Industrial Co-operative stores on Langsett Road c. 1905.

1931 — And Sheffield shows its authority
Dusty Haigh leads attack on the aces

Sheffield Speedway, based in Owlerton, started in 1929 and, apart from the war years, continued until 1952 when the sport went into general decline. However it reopened in 1960 under the promotion of Frank Varey and has continued ever since (apart from two seasons in the 1980s due to promotional problems). This team from 1931 are, right to left: Dusty Haigh, George Corney, Bronco Dixon, Gus Platts, Norman Hartley, Eric Blain, Tommy Allott, -?-.

The 1960 team in the first year back after an eight year lay-off. They are back row, left to right: Jack Winstanley, Stuart Hickman, Malcolm Bruce, Derrol Melbin, Alf Parker. Front row: Tony Robinson, Jack Kitchen.

No section on Hillsborough and Owlerton can be complete without mention of Sheffield Wednesday F.C. The club was formed in 1867 from members of the Sheffield Wednesday Cricket Club. The team played matches at a variety of locations around the city – Hunters Bar, Bramall Lane (!), Olive Grove – but in 1899 they found a permanent home at Hillsborough. They soon acquired the nickname the 'Owls', derived from their connection with Owlerton. This team is the cup winning side of 1935. Back row, left to right: Sharp, Nibloe, Brown, Catlin, Millership, Burrows. Front: Hooper, Surtees, Palethorpe, Starling, Rimmer.

Sheffield Wednesday Division Two Champions 1956. Back row: Froggatt, O'Donnell, Broadbent, McIntosh, McAnearney, Staniforth, Bingley. Front: Jack Marshall (trainer), Gibson, Shiner, McEvoy, Curtis, Finney, Quixall, Eric Taylor.

Alan Finney (left) and Albert Quixall were star wingers for the Wednesday in the 1950s. Quixall left in 1958 to play for Manchester United but Finney stayed at Hillsborough and made over 450 appearances.

Sheffield Wednesday 1902-1903. Top row: W.E. Hemingfield, J. Stewart, T.L. Jarvis, W. Barnett. Middle row: J. Davis, R. Ferrier, A.Langley, J. Lyall, T. Grawshaw, W. Layton, H. Burton, H. Ruddlesden, R. Frith.

Five

Loxley

The Compensation reservior was used to store water piped from Blackburn Meadows. In 1922 a section of the wall gave way and released the stored water into the River Loxley – fortunately no severe damage to persons or property followed.

The break in the wall at Compensation reservoir in 1922.

Stacey Bank cottages at Loxley in 1946 were originally constructed in 1850. The author was born here!

Nags Head Inn at Loxley *c.* 1951.

Thomas Marshall's steam waggon at Loxley in the 1920s. Firebricks and pipes were loaded onto the waggon and despatched to waiting customers at the steelworks in Sheffield. On the back of the waggon are Winston Gillott, -?-, Jack Thorpe; by the cab is Harry Turner while at the front are Raymond and Cyril Robinson.

Workmen from Swifts Rolling mills Storrs Bridge, Loxley. The mill was to close in the 1950s. Back row: Tubby Wilson, Horace Beard, Harry Green, Ernest Twigg. Front: Frank Nicholls, ? Thompson.

The workmen from Thos. Wraggs Refractory works at Loxley in 1925.

SCHOOL-HOUSE. LOXLEY. W.T.F.

The old school and chapel house at Loxley *c.* 1905. This school closed in 1911 after the completion of the newer school in the village. The building has recently been converted into homes after standing derelict for many years.

Loxley School in 1908. This photograph was taken at the old chapel school on Loxley Road which pupils attended prior to the opening of the current Loxley Junior and Infant school in 1911.

Loxley Chapel in 1910. It was built in 1787 and finally closed in 1993 although the burial ground is still in use. A number of graves from victims of the Sheffield flood of 1864 can be found in this yard including members of the Chapman and Armitage families.

The blacksmith's shop at Loxley. Mr Harry Fletcher is shown hard at work on the premises. He had followed his father into the trade and often gave displays and exhibitions of farrier work. He was tragically killed in a traffic accident in 1975 and the business closed shortly afterwards.

A horse team outside the Admiral Rodney at Loxley in 1900. The blacksmith's shop is on the left of this picture.

Loxley Blacksmith's shop *c.* 1910 – at this time the business was owned by the Hardcastle family. The site is now a part of the car park extension for the Admiral Rodney Inn.

Loxley water trough *c.* 1920. There were two sections to the water trough – on the left a small canopy denoted which part was reserved for people while the open end was designated for horses. The stones surrounding the base prevented horses from damaging the trough.

The old Admiral Rodney, seen here in 1910, was demolished in the late 1950s and a new inn constructed on an adjacent field.

The Loxley Post Office in 1910 was built in 1864 as a smallholding complete with workshops. It closed in 1939 and transferred to the current premises three hundred yards further down the road. The building continued to be used as a shop until the early 1960s and is now an animal sanctuary.

Wortley Rural District Aveling and Porter steamroller *The Rolling Monarch* pictured here with the Loxley Valley road team *c*. 1920. Left to right: Harry Walker, George Coldwell, -?-, -?-, Royston Copley, -?-, -?-.

Occupation House at Loxley, seen here c. 1925, was built in 1886 in Occupation Lane (now France Road after construction of the housing estate in the 1940s). The house is now the village shop.

Loxley Junior school in 1933. Back row, left to right: Margaret Crawfold, Eric Gregory, -?-, -?-, Molly Kenyon, Alan Lowe, Lucy Stenton, Joan Wright, James Wood. Top middle row: Phyllis Shaw, Vera Percy, James Wright, -?-, Ruby Williams, Raymond Hague, John Goodison, -?-, -?-. Bottom middle row: Margaret Hague, Mildred Guite, Maureen Billam, Nancy Eyres, Dorothy Hague, -?-, Gwen Barnes. -?-. Front row: Reg Dawson, Wilfred Wood, Albert Wild, Jessie Percy, Derek Nicholson, Ken Hollingsworth, -?-, George Shepherd.

Loxley Junior school 1958. Back row, left to right: Megan Green, Patricia Nicholls, Jean Gregory, Moira Steel, Marilyn Bradwell. Middle row: Malcolm Nunn, Marilyn Westhead, Linda Pontefract, Linda Harper, Brenda Hammond, Desmond Harper, Leslie Pickering. Front row: Philip Sherratt, David Biggin, Kathleen Glossop.

Loxley Institute Cricket Club c. 1930. Back row, left to right: Alwyn Harper, Harry Wright, Luther Baxter, Harry Walker, Arnold Ibbotson, -?-, Jack Baldwin, -?-, Charles Harper, Harold Fretwell. Front row: Robert Copley, Rhoden Elliott, Lol Towers, Alwyn Malinson, Albert Leach, -?-, Billy Wright (centre, front).

Workmen from Little Matlock Rolling mill take a break on the banks of the River Loxley
c. 1905.

Jackson's Cottages on Little Matlock Lane were so named because they were occupied for many years by members of the Jackson family. Sadly these charming cottages were demolished in the 1970s.

Digging for coal at Loxley during the strike of 1912. Loxley is not a coal-mining area but some could be found on the outcrops of the gannister seams. This scene is at Thornwell Bank with Wadsley and Loxley Common in the background.

Thornwell Bank on the Loxley Road in 1910. The Methodist chapel is just visible on the right. The boundary between Sheffield and the West Riding of Yorkshire is a few yards below this point.

Six
Wadsley

Dykes Hall at Wadsley in the 1920s. This fabulous building, whose last resident was R.S. Gowers, was demolished in 1927 to make way for the Wisewood estate.

Wadsley Lane in 1900. Today the open space on the right contains housing.

Horse and Jockey Inn at the junction of Wadsley Lane, Laird Road and Worrall Road. The triangular grassed section on the left is regarded as the Wadsley village green.

Wadsley in 1969 and the junction of Worrall Road and Laird Road. These houses were demolished in the late 1960s for redevelopment.

A view of Wadsley church in 1910.

A charming picture of the junction at Langsett Avenue and Worrall Road *c.* 1905. The large tree in the centre is said to have been stolen from a line of trees in the Middlewood Hospital grounds.

Wadsley National school in 1890. The headteachers at this time were Mr and Mrs Westerman.

Seven

Worrall

Low Ash Hall at Worrall was a private school from 1850 to 1880.

The Yews on the Worrall Road was formerly a childrens home and is now used as a day hospital.

Grange Farm on the Kirkedge Road *c*. 1965 was demolished soon after this picture was taken. On the site today is a housing estate.

Another view of Grange Farm in the mid 1960s.

Worrall Hall was originally the home of Mr Gutteridge the local cobbler. A coat of arms is mounted above the doorway.

Shoulder of Mutton public house in 1910. This view is virtually unchanged. Low farm at the rear was demolished to make way for a car park. The adjoining house, once a private residence, is now part of the inn.

The old shop on Towngate Road was known locally as 'Top Shop' and at one stage was used as the Post Office. These buildings have now been demolished.

Fox House on Top Road was originally called the Brown Cow Inn.

Towngate Road, Worrall c. 1950. These two homes have now been converted into a single residence.

Townside Farm on the Towngate Road was at one time the premises of Walker's butchers shop.

Darren Fold on Towngate Road was demolished in the 1960s and the site rebuilt with modern housing; Wiggan Farm in the background remains unchanged.

Worrall Independent chapel on Towngate Road. The chapel was on the first floor with a school room below.

Worrall Village school closed in the 1960s and the local children were transferred to Oughtibridge. The building is now a private residence.

Blue Ball Inn *c.* 1900 – the building on the far right was a 'Little Mesters' cutlery works.

Haggstones Road looking toward Worrall *c.* 1900. Left to right are the Blue Ball Inn, workers cottages, the chapel and the school.

Gate Bank Farm, known locally as Hayward's Farm, is situated just off Burnt Hill.

Asplands Farm on Boggard Lane *c.* 1950.

Eight
Oughtibridge

A view down Church Street at Oughtibridge *c.* 1950.

At the bottom of Church Street *c*. 1920. On the top right is the Reform chapel, at the bottom of the street is the Wesleyan chapel (now demolished).

Morgan's shop on Church Street *c*. 1900. These premises are today an off-licence.

Jarvill's Dam, just off Church Street at Oughtibridge. The buildings, which once housed a corn mill, have since been demolished but the dam is still there.

COMMON SIDE, OUGHTIBRIDGE

A view from 1910 overlooking Commonside and Church Street. The Parish Hall can be seen behind the line of poplar trees. In the foreground is Kaye Meadow while beyond lies the Don Valley.

The junction of Langsett Road North and Church Street *c.* 1905. Hayward's butchers shop is on the left and the newsagents is on the right.

Langsett Road North at Oughtibridge *c.* 1905. The Langsett Road was originally called New Street. The houses on the right of the road have since been demolished but the White Hart Inn on the left remains.

Bankwell Spring and Poppy Lee's Yard at Oughtibridge *c*. 1910. It was here that Oughtibridge's 'pop' and vinegar manufacturer was based. Each bottle produced here contained a glass marble stopper, a type known as a Codd bottle (after their inventor). The pressure of the gas in the liquid would force the marble against a rubber seal in the neck of the bottle creating a perfect seal.

A view from 1905 down Oughtibridge Lane with the Pheasant Inn just visible on the right.

Station Lane at Oughtibridge *c.* 1925. The railway track in the foreground was used to transport materials from one silica works to another.

The Cook Inn at Bridge Hill (known locally as Cock Hill) *c.* 1905.

Low Road looking towards Oughtibridge *c.* 1920. The River Don flows southwards on the right of the picture. To the left is the Zion chapel.

Middlewood Mill or 'Slitting Mill' *c.* 1930. The mill closed in the 1960s and the site was cleared.

The old Post Office on Langsett Road North *c.* 1910. The building was later used as a chip shop but is now a private residence.

Peter Dixon's steam waggon *c.* 1905. Dixon's were paper manufacturers and were subsequently bought by British Tissues Ltd and then Jamont U.K. (Jamont is now probably the largest employer in the area).

Nine
Ewden Valley
Midhope, Langsett and Brightholmlee

BROOMHEAD HALL.

Broomhead Hall was constructed in 1640, extensively rebuilt in 1840 and then demolished in 1970. For centuries the hall was home to the Remington-Wilson family who still own the surrounding land.

Wigtwizzle Hall was over 400 years old when it was demolished in the 1920s. The stone from the hall was used to build houses for employees of the waterboard following the construction of the Ewden Valley reservoirs.

Dwarriden House was the home of the Ronksley family for 250 years. It was demolished in the late 1920s.

Broomhead Bridge, *c*. 1910. The Ewden Valley was submerged following the construction of the reservoir in the 1920s.

Ewden or New Mill Bridge *c*. 1910. After the construction of the reservoirs the bridge was taken apart and re-assembled in Glen Howe Park at Wharncliffe Side.

A woodland scene overlooking the Ewden Beck.

The reservoir huts at Ewden Valley were built to house the workmen constructing the reservoir during the 1920s. Some of these huts can still be seen today.

High Lea Farm at Brightholmlee is unusual in as much as it is a cruck house – a rare example as most cruck buildings are barns.

Swinnock Hall at Brightholmlee was rebuilt on the site of an older hall dating from 1416 and belonging to the estate of John Swinnock. Later inhabitants of the hall included the Waterhouse and Bradshaw families.

A picturesque view over Brightholmlee just after the turn of the century.

The Manor Farm at Brightholmlee *c*. 1910.

Midhopestone church can trace its origins back to the twelfth century.

LANGSETT RESERVOIR.

Langsett reservoir was constructed at the turn of the century and remains the largest of the original reservoirs in north-west Sheffield.

Ten
The Great Flood
of 1864

On 11 March 1864 at 11.30 p.m. Dale Dyke reservoir embankment burst allowing almost 700 million gallons of water down into the Loxley Valley. The damage was estimated at £500,000 and some 240 people were killed, bodies being found as far away as Doncaster and some were never discovered. The majority of the victims were from Malin Bridge, Hillsborough, Owlerton and Neepsend. Numerous bridges, watermills and properties were simply washed away such was the strength of floodwater. A memorial plaque was dedicated in Bradfield Church on 12 March 1989 and a memorial stone erected on the site of the ill-fated embankment by Bradfield Historical Society in 1991. This scene is of Burnside Cottages at Bradfield – it was here that the first fatality occured when a three day old baby was washed away from its mothers arms.

Roebuck House at Dam Flask. The occupants of these houses had used a leg of their sideboard to smash a hole in the roof to make an escape.

Rowell wheels and house after the flood. The house (now Croft House) was at this time an inn with adjacent wire mill and cutlery works.

The remains of Denton and Chapman's works. This site was rebuilt as Little Matlock Rolling mill. The Riverdale Cottages in the background are virtually unchanged.

A macabre scene of debris at Malin Bridge – many lives were lost in this area.

The Hill Street or Walkley Lane Bridge was damaged but remained unbowed after the flood.

The unveiling of the flood memorial stone on 11 March 1991 by Mr Martin Olive, the former head of Local Studies at Sheffield Central Library.